The

VOODOO REVENGE
Book

An Anger Management Program
You Can Really Stick With

By **MARK SHULMAN**

ILLUSTRATED BY **JOE BARTOS**

Main Street
A division of Sterling Publishing Co., Inc.
New York

Library of Congress Cataloging-in-Publication Data Available

3 5 7 9 10 8 6 4 2

O•MF

Created by Oomf, Inc.

www.Oomf.com

© 2002 by Mark Shulman

Main Street is an imprint of Sterling Publishing Co., Inc.

Published by Sterling Publishing Co., Inc.

387 Park Avenue South, New York, NY 10016

Distributed in Canada by Sterling Publishing

c/o Canadian Manda Group, One Atlantic Avenue, Suite 105

Toronto, Ontario, Canada M6K 3E7

Distributed in Australia by Capricorn Link (Australia) Pty. Ltd.

P.O. Box 704, Windsor, NSW 2756, Australia

Printed in China

Sterling ISBN 1-4027-1231-6

For Brother Theodore.
Of course.

Absolute thanks to Joe Bartos for his outrageous illustrations and superb design sense. I'm also grateful to Eric Doescher for many hours of invaluable, jocose, mordant, and verbose *va et vien* in helping shape this book. Thanks to Greg, Cassia and Dino for getting the project up and running. And Mom, we wouldn't be making those voodoo dolls without your sage advice. As for my dear wife Kara, who was thoroughly pregnant during the whole book-building experience, you are: wonderful.

ABOUT THE AUTHOR

Mark Shulman writes for children and adults.

He is an acclaimed lecturer and infrequent talk show guest on the topic of writing books about Voodoo. Specifically, books that reflect no real knowledge of Voodoo whatsoever.

When not sticking pins in simulated landlords and cab drivers, Mark develops innovative and funny books for Oomf, Inc. Other books by Mark Shulman include *Secret Hiding Places (for Clever Kids)*, *Colorful Illusions*, *How I Built Rusty (and You Can, Too)*, *Fillmore & Geary Take Off!* and several more. He used to be in advertising.

Mark and his wife Kara live in New York.

TABLE OF

CONTENTS

ALL FED UP AND NO PLACE TO GO?

Some people naturally get what's coming to them. For the rest, there's voodoo.

Only *The Voodoo Revenge Book* helps you organize your rage so conveniently. On page after page, you'll find evil, vengeful acts that apply to enemies, friends, and loved ones. Channel the mysteries of the ages directly into the obnoxious, irritating, aggravating people in your life. Enjoy hours and hours of satisfying occult activity at home and work.

The Voodoo Revenge Book was written for beginners, but professionals use it, too. These sacred rituals and chants have been translated and fully updated for the modern household. Any items required can be found in your cupboards and closets. They are just as effective as chicken blood and, quite frankly, don't smell as bad. (We also tried finding chicken blood at the local grocery. Not easy.)

If life doesn't stick it to people the way it should, that's what the little pins are for. They suffer, and you feel better.

> **AUTHOR'S NOTE:** There is a difference between Vodou and Voodoo. "Vodou" is an ancient and respected religion. "Voodoo" is the completely invented concept of going after someone without their knowing it. Don't be fooled by authentic beliefs. It's all about revenge.

HOW TO DO
THAT VOODOO

To make your doll an active revenge partner, help it capture the essence of your victim. There are three general ways to succeed. (Your actual mileage may vary.)

THE MOST EFFECTIVE:
As your defense lawyer will tell you, nothing makes the case like DNA. Touch the doll directly to the victim's hair, skin, bodily fluids... whatever you can stomach. Be brave.

MOSTLY EFFECTIVE:
Personal property (and yes, get personal) should be in contact with the doll for several hours to tenderize it. If it smells like them, all the better. Don't think of it as stealing. Call it research.

ALMOST EFFECTIVE:
Channel your victim by pinning photographs, handwritten notes, and similar objects to the doll. Write the victim's name across its chest. Repeat that person's name over and over in the doll's ear. Show how much you care.

CHANTS, NOT RANTS

Some experts say if you're not chanting over your doll, it isn't voodoo. Who are we to disagree? Chants are provided for each type of victim. Before (and after) you perform a voodoo activity, wave your hands over the doll in a convincing manner. Repeat the chants as often as you think necessary—you'll know when to stop. Don't go overboard.

HOW TO MAKE A
VOODOO DOLL

There is an ancient wisdom passed down among practitioners of voodoo that is brilliant in its simplicity, yet easy to ignore. Without it, true voodoo is almost impossible. We have translated this saying to English as best we can:

"If you burn a doll/And cut it up/And throw it far/ Taped to a Frisbee™/You will soon/Need another."

According to a universal authority on the sacred craft of needlework (the author's mother), here are the basics for making endlessly powerful and effective voodoo dolls of your own. Hi, Mom.

Materials needed:
Sturdy paper, fabric,
scissors, needle, thread,
cotton for stuffing

1 Draw a basic doll outline about 6" high and 5" across its arms. Now cut it out.

2 Trace the form on a piece of fabric. Do it again so you have front and back of the doll. Now cut that out, too.

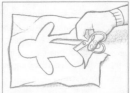

3 Thread needle and knot end of the thread. Starting under left arm of the doll, about 1/4 inch from the edge, *push needle from front of doll to back and pull thread through.

4 Bring needle and thread back up to front of the doll, around 1/4 inch from the last stitch, and pull through.

5 Repeat step 3 from * on.

6 Repeat step 4.

7 Continue in this manner around the edges of the arm, around the head, around the edges of the other arm, down the side of the body, around the edges of both legs. Go up the other side a bit but stop 2 inches away from where sewing began.

8 Stuff the doll with cotton and fill as full as you wish.
[Author's note: It is not necessary to approximate the weight of your victim with cotton.]
[Author's mother's note: Don't interrupt your mother.]

9 Take needle and thread and close the opening in the same way the doll was stitched. Now you may stick it with pins as often as you wish, dear.

STOP SEWING AND STUFF YOUR DOLL HERE

You're standing outside a movie theater. It's the last night to see that film everyone likes (except the critics). It's pouring rain. Your "friend" with the free movie tickets is nowhere in sight. The movie starts in five minutes and rainwater slowly fills your shoes. Through the glass doors you watch happy, dry people buying expensive popcorn. Your cell phone rings: "Hey, I guess I'm running late again. Let's make it another night." The show is sold out. **You want REVENGE!**

DO THAT VOODOO

It's no coincidence that we refer to dead people as "late." These voodoo solutions are right on time.

1 Put a wristwatch around the voodoo doll's heart and fasten it tightly. *[Aligns their ticker with the watch's ticker and forces them to learn to tell time by heart.]*

2 Place doll in salad spinner. Rip a dollar in half and throw it in the spinner on top of the doll. Replace lid and spin furiously. *[Makes them waste money while they always rush to catch up.]*

3 Draw a clock face on the doll's face. Vigorously stick in a circle of 12 pins–one for every hour. *[Imprints a better sense of time upon their brain.]*

4 Arrange your voodoo doll on a plate. Garnish attractively. Place it in the refrigerator for at least one hour. *[Curses them to eat food only after it's gotten cold.]*

5 Light a fire under the doll's feet, then quickly dunk in boiling water. *[Teaches them that if they don't get moving, they'll land in hot water.]*

IF ALL ELSE FAILS...

Pick a time and place to get together. Then don't show up.

CURSE

Tick Tock
Tick Tock
Your master now
Will be the clock
Tock Tick
Tock Tick
Each time you're late
You'll feel real sick

You're on the road, late to work. There's a red car vigorously tailgating you, giving you heartburn and a migraine. Suddenly the car peels out and passes you. The license plate reads HOTSTUF. The driver tosses a can of non-alcoholic beverage out the window, swerves into your lane, then out, then back in again to dodge a truck. Tires squeal, brake lights flash, bumpers crunch. Guess who's insurance has to pay? **You want REVENGE!**

HE BAD DRIVER

DO THAT VOODOO

Bad drivers drive people crazy. Keep your doll handy in the car, and take it out when the feeling moves you.

1 Hold the doll against your mouth. Recite the car's color, model and make, and/or license plate, three times to prepare the doll for voodoo. *[Make sure you don't accidentally voodoo that State Police officer.]*

2 Whack the doll twice against your rear-view mirror, or the turn signals. *[Forces them to use mirrors and signals when they change lanes in front of you.]*

3 Wedge the doll inside a Driver's Education manual. Place it on the driver's seat and sit on it. *[Impresses driving rules upon them.]*

4 Throw the doll on the car floor and step on it. *[Prompts them to step on it.]*

5 Leave the doll under a badly-parked vehicle's windshield wiper for five seconds. *[Attracts parking tickets from police and a bevy of meter maids.]*

6 At home, beat the doll with a tire iron. *[Drives home the anger other drivers feel.]*

IF ALL ELSE FAILS...

Buckle up, buckle down, and just relax.

HEX

Honk Honk Honk Honk
Everything you do is wronk
Beep Beep Beep Beep
Take a driving lesson, creep
Whirr Whirr Whirr Whirr
Pull over pal, your car's a blur
Toot Toot Toot Toot
Next time, take another route

You're home after a long, grueling day. You sit down to a dinner of...gruel. The phone rings. It's a stiff-voiced bill collector. You hang up, and another one calls. Then another. You'd pay if you could. Isn't it the thought that counts? You're already using your overdue notices for placemats and napkins. If they were printed on perforated tissue, they'd be perfect. The door-bell rings. They've come to repossess your vibrating bed. **You want REVENGE!**

THE BILL

COLLECTOR

DO THAT VOODOO

If you're getting behind in your bills, here's how to get that bill collector right in the behind.

1 Strike the doll with the phone repeatedly while they're still on the line. Apologize (if you'd like). Explain that you have a bad connection and hang up. *[Channels their energy into the voodoo doll and gets rid of the call at the same time.]*

2 Pin their return address on doll's head, tie a string around its waist, and whirl it madly around and around. *[Keeps them off-balance so they can't remember your name.]*

3 Wrap the doll in your bills and overdue notices and tape or pin them in place. *[Leaves them in the dark, and makes them think it's all wrapped up.]*

4 Make a tent out of your checkbook and put the doll under it. *[Earns their pity when they see your checking balance.]*

5 Make the doll cozy. Sing the *Bill Collector's Lullaby* to the doll. *[Puts them to sleep every time they try to get in touch with you.]*

IF ALL ELSE FAILS...

Take the phone off the hook.

LULLABY

Rock-a-bye collector
There on the phone
When you call up
There's nobody home
When you send mail
It goes in the trash
I'll pay you tomorrow
If I have the cash

you're getting ready for a really important interview. You need to iron your shirt, but the borrower has your iron. You're a softie when it comes to lending things. Over the past few years, the borrower has dropped by, first for a cup of alphabet noodles, then for one-half the contents of your larder, then the rest of your larder, your lighter and your ladder, and **then** the entire garage. You need the garage back, but not as much as you need that iron. **You want REVENGE!**

THE BORROWER

DO THAT VOODOO

Getting tired of giving so much to so many people? Give yourself a voodoo solution instead.

1 Line a small box with soft cotton or other stuffing and place the doll gently inside. Mail it to yourself. *[Assures they will take care of, and return, the things they borrow.]*

2 Tape the doll to a boomerang. *[Makes them incapable of not returning your things promptly.]*

3 Cut yourself out of a photograph and pin the remaining scraps on the doll. *[Convinces them to go borrow from somebody else next time.]*

4 Pin a dollar to one of the doll's hands and that cut-out photo of you to the other. *[Makes them go out and buy something you really want, and give it to you.]*

5 Put the doll inside an empty wallet. *[Shows them you have nothing they want.]*

6 Tape a magnet to the doll and place the doll wherever your possessions were. *[Makes their returning your items very attractive.]*

IF ALL ELSE FAILS...
Don't answer the door.

CHANT

Borrower, Borrower
Don't ask to borrow
Not today
And not tomorrow
Borrower, Borrower
Leave me alone
Just hit the store
And buy your own

ou're at work and the day is finally over. You're excited. You managed to get a pair of $150 tickets for that sold-out event tonight. For a mere $3,200. Suddenly the boss appears with a pile of work that's due tomorrow. The boss knew about this for weeks, but forgot to tell you. "As long as you're sleeping here tonight," says the boss,"I'll be glad to use those tickets for you." **You want REVENGE!**

DO THAT VOODOO

If you're getting bossed around at work, here's some voodoo that will work for you.

1 Drip twelve drops of Midnight Oil on the doll. *[Forces them to stay until midnight every night, while you actually go home on time.]*

2 Crumple up a shopping list and skewer it to the doll with multiple pins. *[Makes it painful for them to ask you to run personal errands.]*

3 Throw the doll against the ceiling eight times. *[Convinces them to give you a raise eight times a year.]*

4 Wrap a paper clip, binder clips, or a rubber band tightly around the doll's neck. *[Stops them from choking you with extra work.]*

5 Seal the doll inside a company envelope and stamp the word CONFIDENTIAL all over it. *[Keeps their eyes and ears away from your personal communications.]*

IF ALL ELSE FAILS...

Call an employment agency.

CURSE

Hey, Big Shepherd
I'm no sheep
I do the work
While you're asleep
You get the carrot
I get the stick
Time for a change
It's making me sick

You're on a very long train ride on a very short train, enjoying your first vacation in years. Next to you are people who think their kid is perfect. And you agree...perfectly awful. Yelling, whining, running, crying, kicking, shoving—you haven't seen such bad manners since Pro Wrestling. Now the kid seems to be practicing for a yodeling contest with a mouthful of food. Just imagine, only seventeen more hours of this. **You want REVENGE!**

HE BRAT

DO THAT VOODOO

If there's a kid who's making you crazy, these voodoo solutions will make you sane. No kidding.

1 Put a plastic bandage across the doll's mouth. *[Stops them from whining, complaining, and saying anything that will drive you mad.]*

2 Put unpopular food (like broccoli or cauliflower) into a plastic bag with the doll. *[Makes them eat what they're given.]*

3 Glue macaroni to the doll's ears. *[Improves their hearing so they do as they're told.]*

4 Place the doll in a corner of the room. *[Keeps them from being the center of attention.]*

5 Sandwich the doll between two textbooks. *[Straightens them out at school.]*

6 Spank the doll's bottom with a ruler. *[For all the obvious reasons.]*

IF ALL ELSE FAILS...

Put on your sleep-mask and earplugs.

SPELL

Lack of control
Did spoil your child
And that is why
Your child's reviled
Adjust the behavior
From wild to mild
Or Pest Control
Will have to be dialed

You're sitting in a public place, having a private conversation. You're sharing an acid-reflux discussion with that sweetheart who's gone sour. Who gets all the can openers? Who gets the postage stamp collection from Togo? You want to curl up in a fetal position. The butt-insky, who has been listening in without shame, butts in, loudly offering "to make the tough decisions for both of you," and sign you both up for computer dating. **You want REVENGE!**

HE BUTT-INSKY

Do That Voodoo

If someone has their nose in your business, make it your business to know this voodoo.

1 Cover the doll's eyes with black tape. *[Stops them from looking in your private things.]*

2 Attach an alligator clip to each of the doll's ears. *[Prevents them from eavesdropping on your important conversations.]*

3 Fasten the doll's mouth shut with pins. *[Makes them incapable of giving advice.]*

4 Stick a pin in the doll's butt. *[Keeps them from butting in where they're not wanted.]*

5 Light a match over the doll. *[Burns up all their hot air.]*

6 Pound a nail through the doll's mouth. *[Keeps them from talking endlessly about things they don't know about.]*

If All Else Fails...

Use the two magic words: Butt out!

JINX

Hinsky Minsky
Big Butt-insky
You bring itching
On my skin-sky
Hold your tongue
And don't drop in-sky
Or your doll
Will get a pin-sky

23

You're returning home from an unexpected trip to a faraway place. The "friend" who's been watching your home forgets to meet you with the keys. After a 24-hour locksmith breaks down the door, you see how well you've been taken care of. Your sofa is unstuffed. Your car is a cube. Your goldfish is floating in coffee. Your wall-to-wall carpeting no longer lives up to its name. "Okay, okay," says your careless caretaker, "Who knew this stuff meant so much to you?" **You want REVENGE!**

HE CARELESS

Do That Voodoo

If you know people who are careless, you can't afford to be voodoo-less. Here's all the voodoo you could care for.

1 Wrap the voodoo doll in a long sheet of bubble-wrap. *[Prevents them from wrecking your property, plus the added potential for suffocation.]*

2 Put as many pins as possible into the doll, so it looks like acupuncture. *[Increases their sensitivity, so they won't keep hurting people's feelings.]*

3 Put the doll in a bag with a light bulb. Seal the bag and crush the bulb with your foot. *[Improves their memory so these dim bulbs won't forget important things.]*

4 Rub a large eraser over the doll. *[Makes sloppy work vanish, just like that!]*

5 Hold the doll over your head and drop it frequently. *[Teaches them, painfully, the value of being careful with other people's important things.]*

If All Else Fails...

If they're still careless, try to care less.

CURSE

Crash, Tinkle
Slam, Boom
You could wreck
A rubber room
Boom, Slam
Tinkle, Crash
Now you've ruined it
Pay me cash

ou're splurging in a restaurant that's so fancy, you
saved all year just to buy appetizers. As soon as
the snooty waiter delivers your food, a phone at
the next table rings. "Pork bellies are a good investment,"
you hear, very loudly. "Intestines and brains are better.
Hold on, a call's coming in. HOW backed up is my toilet?
Tell the plumber to reach in there and...." **You want
REVENGE!**

HE CELL-PHONE ADDICT

DO THAT VOODOO

If you have to call up all your strength to avoid screaming at public phoners, here are some voodoo solutions that ring true.

1 Wrap the doll in aluminum foil. Bake at 350 degrees for ten minutes. *[Ruins their reception, and gives them heat for taking calls during meals.]*

2 Glue the doll to a toy car and push it off a table. *[Prevents them from dangerous "driving while discussing."]*

3 Burn a movie ticket stub and sprinkle the ashes on the doll. *[Curses them to keep seeing the movie they interrupted over and over again.]*

4 Put ice on the doll's throat. *[Freezes their voice to stop them from yelling personal details into the phone.]*

5 Tie a cell phone to the doll's back. *[Tortures them by being very, very close to a phone they can't use.]*

IF ALL ELSE FAILS...

Call up and cancel their service.

HEX

Your telephone
Has been affected
Telephone number
Disconnected
Take the phone
And don't inspect it
Toss it far
Good work—you wrecked it

You're in a less expensive restaurant this time, but there are six of you. To be speedy and friendly, five of you agree to split the bill evenly. Number Six screams, "No way!" Out come the calculator, the abacus, the math cubes. After hours of long division, the restaurant closes for the night and you get the verdict: The cheapskate just saved thirteen cents. **You want REVENGE!**

HE CHEAPSKATE

Do That Voodoo

People who choke every dollar really need a change. Here's some voodoo you can take to the bank.

1 Tape two small coins over the doll's eyes, then squash the doll in your fold-out sofa. *[Encourages them to pay for a hotel instead of sleeping on your couch.]*

2 Tie the doll's hands to its sides. *[Prevents them from using your things instead of buying their own.]*

3 Take a strand of hair, tie it in a knot and place over the doll. *[Keeps them from splitting hairs when the restaurant tab arrives.]*

4 Put an old dirty penny over the doll's mouth. *[Stops them from arguing about money.]*

5 Dunk the doll upside down in a vase of flowers. *[Reminds them to bring a little something nice when they visit.]*

If All Else Fails...

Next time, forget to bring your wallet.

CHANT

Hey, hey
What do you say?
Next time is your turn to pay
Ooh, ooh
What do you do?
Next time I'll pay
"Next time" too

You're gathered together at home for a friendly board game. Well, almost friendly. One of the players takes three or four turns in a row, stuffs play money up a sleeve, and bankrupts Grandma in a complex swindle. When you come back from the bathroom, you discover the blank piece of paper you signed "as a joke" has become a legally-binding bill of sale. For your car. For ten dollars. **You want REVENGE!**

HE CHEAT

DO THAT VOODOO

If you're tired of people who always finagle more than their fair share, why not share some of this voodoo with them?

1 Cut out the center of an ace of spades. Poke it into the doll's heart like a weapon. *[Ends their cheating at all sorts of games.]*

2 Wrap the doll in an income tax form, and staple it to the doll. *[Attracts the government to audit their income tax frauds.]*

3 Put the doll face down on a scale. Put a quarter on its back. *[Keeps them from over-charging you behind your back.]*

4 Strangle the doll with red tape. *[Stops them from using legal tricks to cheat you out of what's yours.]*

5 Pin a "Go Directly to Jail" card to the doll. *[Reminds them that cheaters not only don't win, they often end up scrubbing prison toilets.]*

IF ALL ELSE FAILS...

Use hidden cameras.

CURSE

There once was a terrible cheat
Who found every victory sweet
But cheaters get caught
And get what they ought
You will feel what it's like to be beat

ou're taking your new computer out of the box. It's the best one you've ever owned. You had to sell all your blood to pay for it. The competitor casually aims a harpoon at your bubble. "Yours is cute. But my computer holds 80 billion gigabytes and has a movie screen for a monitor. It also controls an electronic robot that cleans my house and pays my bills. You paid <u>how much</u> for that little toy? I got mine from NASA, for free." **You want REVENGE!**

DO THAT VOODOO

For people who are always competing to get the best of you, here's the best voodoo to make you the winner.

1 Open a big, heavy dictionary to the word *zyzzyva*, stuff the doll inside, and slam it shut. *[Punishes them for always getting the last word.]*

2 Put a magnifying glass over the doll and leave in the sun until it begins to scorch the doll. *[Burns them with the same scrutiny they use to make you look bad.]*

3 Pin a map to the doll and spin it around. *[Stops them from thinking they always know the best way.]*

4 Stick the doll upside down in fine sand. *[Lets them pay the price of wanting the finest things for themselves.]*

5 Tie a string to the doll and drag it behind you. Or better, behind your car. *[Keeps them from getting ahead of you.]*

IF ALL ELSE FAILS...

Buy a used limousine. They cost less than you think.

JINX

Yours is bigger
Yours is better
We both see sunsets
But yours is redder
You claim the most
The very best
But like the emperor
You're undressed

ou're back at the factory, making skeletons for medical schools and "private collectors." There's a quota. You're working overtime, you're underpaid, and bone tired. But your co-worker spends ten minutes working between half-hour breaks. While you try to keep everything moving, lazybones is humming, eating, gabbing, dozing. Guess who got promoted to the head office? Not you—you're always behind in your job. **You want REVENGE!**

HE CO-WORKER

Do That Voodoo

If you want your co-workers to earn their keep, keep using these workable voodoos.

1 Write "Do your work!" on sticky notes and cover the doll with them. *[Gets them to do their job without constant reminders.]*

2 Crush the doll under a paperweight. *[Makes them carry their weight, and get back to work.]*

3 Break a cigarette and/or a potato chip or pretzel over the doll. *[Makes them take less cigarette and/or snack breaks, and get back to work.]*

4 Tape the back of the doll against a clock. *[Gets them to stop watching the clock, and get back to work.]*

5 Whack the doll with a belt buckle. *[Gets them to buckle down, and get back to work.]*

If All Else Fails...

Contact the HR representative nearest you.

SPELL

Hi-ho, hi-ho
It's off to work you go
You will not stop
Until you drop
Hi-ho, hi-ho-hi-ho
Hi-ho, hi-ho
It's back to work you go
My work you'll do
And I'll be through
Hi-ho, hi-ho-hi-ho, hi-ho

You're cooking a nice dinner in your all-electric kitchen. You've spent the day shopping, cleaning, getting ready. This is a meal to be proud of. Now it's time to eat. Guess what? "Hey, why is dinner late? The fork is dirty. Where's my drink? The food's cold. The room's cold. I'm cold. This isn't what I usually eat. And what is this anyway? It's disgusting!" **You want REVENGE!**

Do That Voodoo

Getting tired of all the criticism? This powerful voodoo is nothing to complain about.

1 Stick knitting needles in the dead center of the doll. *[Affects their ability to nitpick at every little thing.]*

2 Twist the head of the doll 180 degrees and hold it while counting to ten. *[Distracts them from what you're doing, so they can't make comments.]*

3 Put the doll inside a bag of sugar and shake energetically. Throw a lemon out the window. *[Encourages them to offer sweet compliments instead of tart criticism.]*

4 Take a pair of pliers and twist the doll's nose. *[Keeps their nose out of other people's business.]*

5 Place the doll in a jar and tighten the lid. Use glue if necessary. *[Shuts them up altogether.]*

If All Else Fails...

Make a tape of their greatest hits, and play it back to them.

CHANT

Icky, icky
You're crit-icky
What makes you
So downright picky?
Here's a real slick
Magic trick:
Things you hate?
I'll make them stick!

ou're working at a small retail store during the big busy season. A customer with a face like a bulldog is holding up the line, demanding items that don't have anything to do with your store. You try a smile. It doesn't work. "Don't you have anything better? Newer? Cheaper? Greener?" If they don't think you're listening, here's what you hear: "I'm reporting you to your boss!" **You want REVENGE!**

HE **CUSTOMER**

DO THAT VOODOO

Service with a smile is sometimes a challenge. Here's some voodoo that guarantees a smile on your face.

1 Punch a hole in each of the doll's hips, and place a drop of oil in the holes. *[Makes it easier for them to part with their cash.]*

2 Stick a pin in the doll's throat, then turn the doll over and over. *[Stops them from complaining, over and over.]*

3 Cover the doll in velvet and pass it quickly over a candle flame. *[Gives them a warm and fuzzy feeling about you.]*

4 Take each of the doll's hands and cut off the fingertips. *[Gets them to leave bigger tips.]*

5 Dunk the doll in a bowl of plain vanilla ice cream. *[Keeps them from making special demands.]*

IF ALL ELSE FAILS...

Tell them, loudly, their credit card was rejected.

JINX

Customer, customer
I've got it rough
Dealing with you
Is torture enough
Customer, customer
Go hit the street!
Leave me your money
And take no receipt

You're home alone, enjoying leftover leftovers in peace and quiet. The phone rings. It's buried under torn photographs, torn letters, torn clothes and books and once you find it, you answer just in time. It's the ex. It's clear the only way to have saved that relationship would have been a complete personality transplant. Then the threats come again: "Police! Lawyer! Psychiatrist! Dog Catcher!" Click. Your blood pressure reads like the temperature of the sun. **You want REVENGE!**

DO THAT VOODOO

When true love becomes a true lie, here's some voodoo that's truly gratifying.

1 Write "void" on one of your checks and tape it to the doll. *[Prevents them from getting any of your money.]*

2 Bang the doll on the head with a telephone receiver. *[Discourages bitter phone calls, and improves their reception to your point of view.]*

3 Cut the doll in half. Put one half in each shoe. Take a walk. *[Lets them feel what it's like to be in your shoes, for a change.]*

4 Lay the doll in a shoebox, then leave it outdoors. *[Keeps them alone, out in the cold, unable to tell any more stinking, lousy lies to your friends.]*

5 Pin your photo on the doll's heart. *[Makes them want to come back.]*

IF ALL ELSE FAILS...

Write a "personals" ad. Or three.

CURSE

Our love is done
That much is true
But here's some fun
I'll have with you
Forever this curse
Will totally
Give you worse
Than you give me

You're all set to watch the Olympics on TV. The food's ready. The phone's turned off. The doorbell's ringing. Oh, no! Your uninvited "guest" strolls in, bringing nothing but a thirst, and then sits in your favorite chair. "Hey, let's watch us some curling!" Soon you're hearing "What's for snacks?" and then "Buuuurp!"

The Olympics end twelve days later, and guess who's still there? **You want REVENGE!**

HE FREELOADER

DO THAT VOODOO

How do you avoid the visitor of your nightmares? Here's some voodoo that's a real dream.

1 Tie an egg timer to the back of the doll. *[Trains them to limit their visits to three minutes.]*

2 Cut open the doll, insert a coin in its stomach, and pin it closed. *[Stops them from eating food they didn't pay for.]*

3 Hang the doll on the wall facing your refrigerator, and hit it on the stomach with a fork. *[Keeps them away from your food.]*

4 Shake the doll vigorously in the direction of their home while chanting the spell. *[Makes them realize they've overstayed their welcome, and must go home.]*

5 Slam your front door on the doll. *[Really makes them realize they've overstayed their welcome, and must go home.]*

IF ALL ELSE FAILS...

Mail them a false "change of address" form.

SPELL

Nobody's home
Nobody's home
Turn around
And leave me alone
I'll make you see
I'll make you see
This hotel's
Got no vacancy

ou're at the office, trying very hard to care about your particular industry. The gossip in the next cubicle is back on the phone, whispering so you can barely hear. "Listen to this juicy news. You'll never believe who might get fired. Here's a hint: bad breath, bad hair, bad clothes, (a pause), mm-hmm, and those hideous orange shoes all the time." Orange shoes??? They're talking about YOU!!! **You want REVENGE!**

HE GOSSIP

DO THAT VOODOO

They say gossip is the devil's something-or-other. It's true. This voodoo will really give them something to talk about.

1 Paint the doll's face bright red. *[Gets them caught doing something embarrassing.]*

2 Drip candle wax over the doll's entire head. *[Seals their gossiping mouths and ears shut forever.]*

3 Pin a piece of cloth to the doll. Then burn the cloth. *[Stops them from inventing stories out of whole cloth.]*

4 Soak the doll in 100% grape juice and wring dry. *[Takes the juice out of their juicy stories, and makes them purple with rage.]*

5 Wrap the doll in packing tape. Put a postage stamp on it. *[Gets them moved to a faraway city where they don't know anybody to talk about.]*

IF ALL ELSE FAILS...

Tell them a false rumor about the boss, and hope the boss hears it.

CHANT

Chit chat
Chit chat
Chit chat
Chit chat
Chit chat
Chit chat
STOP!!!

ou're enjoying a sunny day at the beach. You're happily making sand castles. But the big grouch on the next beach towel is complaining again. "Why is it so hot? Why do people blast radios at the beach? Why do they laugh so loud? Why don't they just shut up?" In a tantrum, the grouch covers both ears and rolls over, flattening your castle and denting your bucket with the starfish on it. **You want REVENGE!**

DO THAT VOODOO

When you've had it *up to here* with that grouch over there, here's a little voodoo you can use right here.

1 Dip the doll's head first into a bowl of ice water, then put it in the freezer overnight. *[Makes them less hotheaded.]*

2 Smear honey all over the doll and put it in a sunny window. *[Puts them in a warm, sweet mood.]*

3 Tie a slipknot in a piece of clothesline and put it over the doll's head. Pull both ends as hard as you can. *[Takes away their voice, so they can't complain all the time.]*

4 Sprinkle salt on the doll, then shake it off. *[Stops them from assaulting you (and giving you the shakes).]*

5 Forget the pins. Drive a nail through the doll's belly. *[Gives them something to be genuinely grouchy about.]*

IF ALL ELSE FAILS...

Sing a bouncy pop song to drown them out.

HEX

Learn to sing
Learn to dance
Remove that burr
From your underpants
Don't be dour
Don't be dank
Together we'll laugh
All the way to the bank
(And you'll give me your money)

You're doing a big favor: driving a set of Siamese twins to the airport at five in the morning. It's pouring rain. Traffic is terrible, and moving slowly. Very slowly. You make a wrong turn and the police give you a traffic ticket. The clock is ticking. The twins are chewing each other's fingernails. You reach the airport just in time. The twins tumble out. "Hey, we almost missed our plane. And don't expect us to pay your tickets," they say, as you get towed from the red zone. You want REVENGE!

HE INGRATE

DO THAT VOODOO

If you know someone who should join a band called "The Ingrateful Dead," here's some voodoo that really rocks.

1 Stick the doll with thorns from the stem of a rose. *[Reminds them to use flowers to express their gratitude.]*

2 Tape a party favor to the doll. Tie the doll to a string of rubber bands. Throw it out the window, bungee-style. *[Makes them return the favor now and then.]*

3 Pin a $50 bill on the doll, with the image of President Grant facing downward. *[Gets them to stop taking you for granted.]*

4 Whack the doll several times with the heel of your shoe. *[Shows them how big a heel they have been.]*

5 Place the doll in a "Thank You" card. Mail it to yourself, first class. *[Gives them a first-class lesson in showing appreciation.]*

IF ALL ELSE FAILS...

Stop going out of your way for them. What's the use?

CURSE

It's true
That you
Have no idea
What I do for you
So please
On your knees
Say "Thanks, thanks, thanks"
Until you wheeze

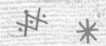

HOW TO VOODO

You're barely awake, trying to get dressed for work in the dark at 4 a.m. On the way to the bathroom you trip over six enormous pieces of luggage, eleven unfamiliar (and loud) new toys, a gift fruitcake that's still in its wrapper, a cookbook inscribed, "Maybe one of these will help?" and the bestseller, <u>Empowering Your Child to Choose a Better Spouse Next Time</u>. Guess who's still in the guest room? **You want REVENGE!**

DO THAT VOODOO

If your in-laws are making you think like an outlaw, this voodoo can save you plenty on lawyers' fees.

1 Cut two days from a calendar, burn in a bowl, and stir the ashes with the doll. *[Confines them to visits that are only two days long. Works with one day, too.]*

2 Bite the doll. *[Reminds them not to leave their false teeth in the bathroom.]*

3 Take a bottle of a drink that can be stored indefinitely, and pummel the doll with it. *[Reduces their chances of spoiling the grandchildren.]*

4 Put the doll's head in a can. *[Causes advice they give you to echo back to them.]*

5 Wrap the doll in a towel and pin it up. *[Prevents them from exposing their strange habits.]*

IF ALL ELSE FAILS...

Stay at their house for as long as possible. Be just as annoying.

SPELL

I know you raised
Your child well
And that's why we got married
But now I'm crazed
You've just been hell
Back off! Or you'll get buried

ou're all dressed up in your favorite dress-up clothes. You've checked yourself out in the mirror, and you're looking fine. It's a beautiful day...or it was, until you heard a nasty voice. "I didn't know you liked vintage clothes," says the insulter. "What vintage is it? I heard you were down in the dumps lately. I guess that's where you got your clothes." The only thing worse than being cursed with an insulting stand-up comedian in your life is being cursed with one who isn't funny. **You want REVENGE!**

HE INSULTER

DO THAT VOODOO

When they say insult, do you think assault? Then pepper them with this well-seasoned voodoo.

1 Bounce the doll against the wall seven times. *[Provides the ability to return the insult every day of the week.]*

2 Put the doll on a lightning rod and leave it outside during a storm. *[Prevents them from saying shocking things to thunderous effect.]*

3 Pin a fortune cookie into the doll's mouth. *[Stops them from saying cruel things in the name of "honesty."]*

4 Wrap the doll in bathroom tissue. *[Gets them caught at an embarrassing moment.]*

5 Bang the doll's head on the counter. *[Helps you come back with a counter insult...next time.]*

6 Tear the doll in half, then dip each end in salt. *[Lets you add injury to insult.]*

IF ALL ELSE FAILS...

Pretend you don't hear them. It sometimes works.

JINX

Sticks and stones
Can break my bones
But names can never hurt me
And sticks and stones
Will break your bones
It's wise if you avert me

You're in the world's largest shoe store. You need special polish for your special shoes. You bring a can to the checkout. Wrong move. "Hey," says the clerk in a very loud voice that hundreds can hear. "Ya totally screwed up here. Ya need Type 14-B for that razzle-dazzle shine. This is 14-A! You wanna wreck those shoes? Go back and get the right polish!" You slink away, your face as red as the polish you selected. **You want REVENGE!**

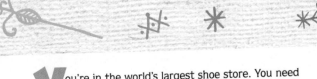

Do That Voodoo

They may think they know a lot, but you can show them the voodoo that's on your mind.

1 Stick a pea to the doll's head with a pin. *[Reduces their brains to pea brains.]*

2 Write "Um" on the doll's face with a brightly-colored lipstick. *[Condemns them to say "um" between every word, damaging their credibility.]*

3 Place the doll in a shoebox with shredded newspaper and shake vigorously. *[Confuses their facts and keeps them in the dark.]*

4 Beat an egg, then dip the doll's head in the goo. *[Leaves them with egg on their face whenever they try to sound important.]*

5 Draw a clown face on the doll. *[Prevents them from making you look foolish in their presence.]*

If All Else Fails...

Respond to any obnoxious comments by reciting endless **useless facts.**

CHANT

*Z,Y,X,W,V,U,T,S,R,Q,P,O,N,M,
L,K,J,I,H,G,F,E,D,C,B,A
Get all your facts backwards today.*

HOW TO VOODO

You're doing your laundry, trying to wash a lot of clothes with a little detergent, when the phone rings. It's your "lender" (who used to be your "friend"), calling for the fifteenth time today. "I was thinking, maybe you could come over and wash all the windows up here in the penthouse. And clean my cat's litter box? I mean, just until you pay me back." You're thinking about payback, all right. **You want REVENGE!**

HE LENDER

DO THAT VOODOO

If you feel like your lender is living on borrowed time, here's some voodoo to balance the scales.

1 Scrub the doll's head in soapy water, then wring it dry. *[Cleanses their brain of any memory of what you owe them.]*

2 Tickle the doll, stroke the doll, and say nice things to it. *[Charms them to completely forgive your debt because you're such a great person.]*

3 Cut off the doll's arms, then toss it on the floor. Stomp on it. *[Makes it impossible for them to collect high interest from you.]*

4 Wrap the doll's head entirely with tape. *[Forces them to shut up about your debt in front of others.]*

5 Tie the doll to a model airplane and toss it out the window. *[Makes it suddenly necessary for them to move too far away to get back whatever you borrowed.]*

IF ALL ELSE FAILS...

Lend them something you don't need, to even the score.

SPELL

When you give
You ought to give
(Without attaching string)
So now you'll find
I've erased your mind
(I don't owe you a thing)

You're standing in the driveway, looking your car up and down. You don't recall getting that scratch. You remember filling the fuel tank. And last you knew, the car had two front fenders. This could only be the work of one person. "Who, me?" whines the liar. "I would never take your car without permission. In fact, I tore up my driver's license after that incident with the ice cream truck." You want more than a new fender. **You want REVENGE!**

HE LIAR

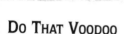

DO THAT VOODOO

If you know people who lie like a rug, this voodoo will throw them and call them on the carpet.

1 Squeeze the doll hard against a credit card, until the numbers are impressed on the doll's head. *[Forces them to take credit for their mistakes, and also tell the truth about money.]*

2 Pass the head of the doll face down through a candle flame. Then dunk it in water. *[Makes them see the light and learn the cold facts about burning people.]*

3 Wrap the doll in a calendar page and stick pins through it. *[Compels them to keep commitments and stick to plans.]*

4 Stick the doll on a rotisserie and let it slowly roast. *[Cures them from going around bragging with all that hot air.]*

5 Drive a big tent stake through the doll's mouth. *[Convinces them rumors and lies are a big mistake.]*

IF ALL ELSE FAILS...

Presume everything they say is a lie. You'll probably be right.

CURSE

Liar, liar, pants on fire
Time to set your ethics higher
Or I'll set your pants on fire

You're lying in bed counting sheep. Does it work? Bah.
What about goats? Naah. Why can't you sleep? Your
neighbors are having a party for everyone who
shares their page in the phone book. Suddenly, a very loud
riding mower makes a very loud crash through a very large
window: yours. "Oops," yells your neighbor, as a form of
apology. The next day, you pay
for the window just by
returning all the
deposit bottles
on your lawn.
**You want
REVENGE!**

DO THAT VOODOO

If you're having a bad time in the City of Good Neighbors, here's some voodoo that should hit close to home.

1 Stick a pin in each of the doll's eyes. *[Keeps them from snooping around your home.]*

2 Throw the doll on the floor and sweep it around the room with a broom. *[Gets them to clean up after themselves in the neighborhood.]*

3 Slam the door on the doll, drop furniture on it, or walk on it. *[Stops upstairs neighbors from all that aggravating behavior.]*

4 Burn a handful of leaves, grass, or other offending natural items and smear the doll with the ashes. *[Prevents all crimes related to lawn and garden.]*

5 Stuff the doll between your mattress and box spring. *[Compels them to go to bed early and stop making loud noises at bedtime.]*

IF ALL ELSE FAILS...

Knock on the door and join the party.

HEX

No sound, no light
No overzealous lovers' fight
No pets, no teens
No Sunday morning lawn machines
No trash, no can
No nothing but a moving van

You're throwing your weekly "T.G.I. Tuesday" party. It's in full swing. The deep fried brussels sprouts are a big hit. The bathtub is just brimming with guacamole. The stereo's blowing fuses. Your front door was removed to appease the Fire Marshall, but it's the police who come visiting this time. Two hours later, when your cop-calling neighbors stroll over to complain in person, they scream, they yell, they tell the police to get dressed and leave before judging the Samba contest. **You want REVENGE!**

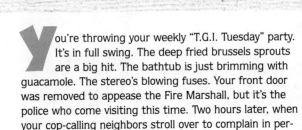

HE PARTY
POOPER

DO THAT VOODOO

If you're a firecracker surrounded by duds, here's some voodoo that's a real blast.

1 Drip birthday candle wax slowly across the doll's face. *[Forces them to patiently endure your fun, and keeps them from finding out where the good times are.]*

2 Cut a photographic negative into several pieces and pin each one to the doll. *[Keeps them from being so darned negative all the time.]*

3 Staple the doll to a blanket. Wet the blanket. Then dry out the blanket. *[Helps you deal with a "wet blanket."]*

4 Sew a tattle-tail on the back of the doll with spare cloth. *[Conditions them never to report people to the authorities again.]*

5 Fit the doll with a party hat, cake, and your drink of choice. *[Teaches them to lighten up and have a good time.]*

IF ALL ELSE FAILS...

Have your next party for mimes only.

CHANT

For fun, you're the worst
Your lips always pursed
In misery immersed
Complaining comes first
(I'm sure you rehearsed)
For each bubble you burst
You'll find yourself cursed

You're right in the middle of your favorite video, <u>How Chinese Checkers Changed the World</u>, when the phone rings. You know who it is. The pest seems to interrupt every single time. "So, how's your family? How's your job? Have you seen the weather report lately?" And then the real reason for the call: to tell you every last detail of a very boring life. You fight the urge to be rude, but you're burning with rage. The VCR, which has been on "pause," has chewed up your video. **You want REVENGE!**

DO THAT VOODOO

When your life is infested by an annoying pest, here is some voodoo that will clip their wings and take out the sting.

1 Place the doll under a telephone book. Step on the book. *[Gets them to forget your phone number and stop calling.]*

2 Make a much smaller voodoo doll and put it in the big doll's arms. *[Helps them get a life of their own, even if it's a tiny one.]*

3 Bind the arms to the body with string. *[Hexes them to keep their hands to themselves.]*

4 Whack the doll with a fly-swatter. *[Makes them aware of how much they are bothering you, and stop.]*

5 Hang the doll from an outside doorknob. *[Keeps them away from your place.]*

6 Mail the doll to Hungary in a boot. *[It's the fastest way to boot a pest.]*

IF ALL ELSE FAILS...

Screen your calls, screen your mail, and use the peephole.

JINX

I protest
To the unwanted guest
You're too obsessed
You leave me stressed
With rage suppressed
And so distressed
I can't digest
This curse I'll test
It leaves you undressed
And under arrest

You're walking down your street toward home, pushing a baby carriage and humming a lullaby. You step in something awful. The culprit, a fast and nasty dog, lunges toward you, chasing a faster and nastier cat. The cat stops, scratches you, hisses, and runs off. The dog stops, bites you, sniffs your shoe, and flees. The dog's leash snags the baby carriage, and starts to pull it away. You yell, "My baby!" The dog owner yells, "My puppy!" When you finally get your baby, safe and sound, the dog owner reports you to the Humane Society. **You want REVENGE!**

DO THAT VOODOO

Whether you want to control the pet owner or the pet, here's some voodoo that will do new tricks for you.

1 Place the doll in a plastic bag with a pair of plastic gloves and a newspaper. *[Gets them to clean up after their pets.]*

2 Put a collar around the doll's neck and cinch it tightly. *[Stops owners from asking you to babysit their beasts; stops beasts from making noise.]*

3 Dip the doll in soapy water, rinse, and wring dry. *[Helps smelly pets get washed now and then.]*

4 Pin the doll's hands to the doll's legs, forcing it into a sitting position. *[Makes pets obey, and makes owners enroll them in obedience school.]*

5 Spray the doll with "Pet Scat" or any nationally-advertised brand of aerosol repellent. *[Gets the pet and its owner to stop shedding, scratching furniture, aggravating you, and otherwise being an animal.]*

IF ALL ELSE FAILS...

Get yourself a pet and join the fun.

HEX

Sit up, lie down
Shake, roll over
Leash and hush
That Kitty and Rover
Chase that ball
Stand on your head
Curb your pet
Or you'll play dead

You're at the butcher shop, waiting patiently near the organic organs. You take a number. Yours is number 420. The butcher calls 37. You hear a petty little voice pipe up. "I'd like eleven chicken gizzards. No, that's twelve. And a pound of liver from a three-year-old cow. And a little hamburger." And then, as the butcher is weighing three ounces of hamburger, out comes a petty little scale. "Weigh it on mine," says the petty. "You see? Mine is correct. I want a discount." You've been waiting an hour already. **You want REVENGE!**

Do That Voodoo

If someone who's pretty petty makes you feel like a patsy, this voodoo makes them putty in your hands.

1 Split a hair down the middle and place it on the doll's heart. *[Stops them from splitting hairs on minor issues, and makes them take the big ones to heart.]*

2 Wrap tape around the doll's fingers or hands. *[Makes them incapable of keeping score against you all the time.]*

3 Tape the doll face-first to a magnifying glass. *[Shocks them into seeing how foolish their tiny thoughts look to others.]*

4 Stick several pins into the doll's head (but don't count them), then slap the doll five times with a yardstick. *[Makes them less of a stickler for trivial rules.]*

5 Stuff the doll into a jar full of small change. *[Teaches them to bottle up their nickel-and-dime behavior.]*

If All Else Fails...

Take your toys and go home.

SPELL

Pity, pity, petty pet
Teeny, teeny, tiny fret
Yammering and yelling, yet
Foolish figments NOW FORGET!

HOW TO VOODOO

You're done waiting—you're finally getting that big promotion at work. You were promised that you'd climb the ladder IF you did all your work AND took 39 classes AND cleaned the photocopier every night AND carried the boss's golf clubs AND kept those clubs nice and shiny. Now it's the big day, but when you open the envelope a little pink slip comes fluttering out. On the back, in the boss's handwriting: "I changed my mind. Bye." **You want REVENGE!**

HE PROMISE BREAKER

DO THAT VOODOO

When you're dealing with people who can't keep their word, here's some voodoo that keeps them honest. We promise.

1 Pin the doll's hands and feet to a wall calendar. *[Makes them stick to commitments and plans.]*

2 Tie several knots in a piece of string, then tie the string tightly around the waist of the doll. *[Subjects them to a string of broken promises worse than they've given anyone else.]*

3 Cut off the doll's fingers or hands. *[Stops them from crossing their fingers to cancel a promise.]*

4 Fill a cup or bowl with salt-water. Stick the doll in, head first. *[Condemns them to drown in the tears of all the people they disappoint.]*

5 Draw an X on the doll's heart, then destroy the doll completely. *[Lets their promise of "Cross my heart and hope to die" come true.]*

IF ALL ELSE FAILS...

Promise yourself never to get suckered again.

CURSE

Open your mouth
And close your eyes
And you will get
A big surprise
You made a promise
For goodness's sake
And like your promise
Your tongue will break

You're at the mechanic's garage, getting new treads for your army tank. You've got the bill in your hand and you're livid. $17,000 for a new turret? You didn't ask for a new turret. "Had to change it," says the mechanic with deliberate slowness. "Them shells weren't hitting the target." You demand to see the old turret, but he says the army guys hauled it away. "Had to call in the Reserves," he says. "And that's gonna cost you, too." **You want REVENGE!**

HE RIP-OFF

Do That Voodoo

Whenever people decide to take what's yours, here's some voodoo that gives them theirs, big-time.

1 Smash the doll's back against the wall, over and over. *[Forces them to give back whatever they took.]*

2 Using the doll, sweep a handful of loose change off the table onto the floor. *[Helps the offending business go bankrupt.]*

3 Wrap the doll in your insurance policy and stick a pin through the heart. *[Inspires the insurance company to pay for your loss, thanks to your sad story.]*

4 Burn the doll's hands with hot wax or a soldering iron. *[Burns and brands the hands of the thief.]*

5 Strangle the doll with a computer cable. *[Crashes the computers of online frauds.]*

6 Cut the doll open, fill it with coins, and then shake out the coins. *[Makes them give you a full refund.]*

If All Else Fails...

Call the Better Business Bureau. Or the cops.

JINX

Your heart's a clamp
Your soul's a curve
Your hands take things
They don't deserve
Stuff everything
You've ever stolen
Up your nose
Until it's swollen

You're home at last, after a day so terrible our publisher won't let us describe it. Sufficient to say, you need a shower. Immediately. You knock politely on the door of the bathroom, but it takes your roommate an hour to finish. When you finally get in, you find your razor dull, your shampoo gone, your soap covered in hair. And that's just the bathroom. The kitchen...well, the publisher won't let us describe that, either. **You want REVENGE!**

DO THAT VOODOO

If your roommate is moving in on your turf, here's the voodoo equivalent of barbed wire.

1 Bat the doll around the room with a broom. *[Forces them to clean up after themselves.]*

2 Snuff out a candle with the doll's head. *[Helps them keep quiet, especially at night. Don't let the doll catch fire, or they'll scream until dawn.]*

3 Draw an X on the doll, and hang it by the neck to the outside doorknob. *[Keeps them out of the house when you need it to yourself.]*

4 Isolate the doll in a plastic container. *[Keeps them from having their friends over, or dating yours.]*

5 Pin the doll's hands behind its back. Rub its face in your food, your clothing, your shampoo, your CDs, your nose hair clippers, your car wax, your...you get the idea. *[Stops them from taking your stuff without asking.]*

IF ALL ELSE FAILS...

Check the want ads.

JINX

Little pig, little pig
Don't come by
My room is clean
And yours: a sty
You've made an awful
Mess around here
Move out tomorrow
Pay rent all year

ou're giving a tour of the United Nations. The tourists are gathered after buying souvenirs for world peace, and you have a heckler in the crowd. You hear the same rude voice in the tour group interrupt your talk at every turn—making dumb jokes (that aren't really jokes) and pointed asides (that aren't really asides) to anyone who will listen (which isn't really anyone). You've been through a lot already. Everyone is embarrassed. You're shaken and stirred. If only the jokes were funny. **You want REVENGE!**

DO THAT VOODOO

If you're dealing with diamonds-in-the-rough, here's some high-pressure voodoo to add a little polish.

1 Wrap electrical tape tightly around the doll's brain. *[Forces them to keep their shocking thoughts to themselves.]*

2 Take dental floss or fishing wire and turn the doll into a marionette. *[Gets them to act more appropriately.]*

3 Place the doll face down on a mirror. *[Makes them take a long, hard look at themselves.]*

4 Hit the doll several times on the head with a musical instrument. *[Prevents them from hitting the same annoying note with their comments.]*

5 Sprinkle the doll liberally with household cleanser. Moisten and use as a sponge. *[Cleans up their humor, and your kitchen.]*

6 Blow up a balloon until it's full. Hold it over the doll's face, then release the air slowly. *[Gives them a taste of someone else's hot air, for a change.]*

IF ALL ELSE FAILS...

Run, don't walk, to the nearest exit.

HEX

You're terribly rude
You always intrude
Stupidity spewed
And you're not very shrewd
May you always get sued
By the people you've stewed
Let your comments be booed
And your tongue shampooed, dude

You're at your high school reunion and you hardly recognize anyone. They've all changed: stomachs are moving forward, hairlines are moving back. But suddenly, you identify the most selfish kid in class. Cutting in the lunch line. Saving seats for "the gang." Upstaging you in the school play. Stuffing the ballot box for Team Mascot. It all comes rushing back. And nothing has changed. That selfish bum is now making a move on your date. **You want REVENGE!**

DO NOT PICK SMELL OR LOOK AT THE FLOWERS!

HE SELFISH

DO THAT VOODOO

If you know people who only take, take, take, then here's the best voodoo to give, give, give.

1 Cut out a color picture of someone—anyone—and pin it to the back of the doll's head. *[Gets them to finally think of someone—anyone—other than themselves.]*

2 Pin the head of the doll to its butt. *[Gets them to see themselves the way others see them.]*

3 Tear a slit in each of the doll's hips. Pass a rolled up dollar bill through the slits, and back out again. Put it in a cup. *[Opens their pockets and pries out a little money for charity.]*

4 Cut off the doll's hand. Keep it in your pocket, or give it to a person of your choosing. *[Forces them to stop grabbing all their toys, and lend a hand to others.]*

5 Whack the doll with a hammer. *[Just feels good.]*

IF ALL ELSE FAILS...

Keep whacking the doll with a hammer.

CHANT

Me, me, me, me
Me, me, me
All you say is
Me, me, me
You, you, you, you
You, you, you
Serving me
Is what you'll do

ou're at the video store, stocking up for a holiday weekend. The in-laws (see page 50) are coming in ten minutes. You're tenth in line. The video clerk moves like a turtle, if at all—typing requests with one finger. Chatting with the cutie at the microwave popcorn concession. Throwing paper basketballs into the trash. C'mon, c'mon, you think, or else it's a weekend of small talk. Time's up. You're stuck with <u>Knitting a Bowling Ball Bag: The Step-by-Step Video</u>. **You want REVENGE!**

HE SLACKER

DO THAT VOODOO

If you know a slacker who's not living up to potential, here's some potentially motivating voodoo to do.

1 Pass the butt of the doll over a candle flame. Then submerge it in ice water. *[Lights a fire under their lazy bottoms and subjects them to life's cold reality.]*

2 Inflate a balloon. Tie it to the doll's head with a strand of hair. Then pop it. *[Bursts the bubble of hair-brained notions and get-rich-quick schemes.]*

3 Beat the doll with an alarm clock seven times. *[Gets them out of bed at seven in the morning. Alter beatings to match desired time.]*

4 Sand the doll with sandpaper, then finish it with varnish. *[Grinds down unrealistic expectations of rewards, and compels them to finish what they start.]*

5 Stick "help wanted" ads to the doll with pins. *[Forces them to find a job, or at least a better one.]*

IF ALL ELSE FAILS...

Yell. Scream. Whatever.

CURSE

Mary had a little lamb
It loved to sleep and snack
One day when Mary had to scram
The lamb did laze and slack
The big bad wolf came strolling by
With jelly made of mint
Now Mary's friend's a mutton pie
I hope you get the hint

you're visiting the kind of relatives who can only be labeled as "distant." Or should be. The head of the household works "in films"—as a consultant for college fraternity movies. This might explain why your feet stick to the kitchen floor. Or why your plate sticks to the table. Or...never mind. When dinner is finally over, you take your dish into the kitchen, where the slob's dog is licking a dish clean. The dish goes straight back to the cupboard. **You want REVENGE!**

LARD

HE SLOB

DO THAT VOODOO

If you're plagued by the terminally messy, here's some voodoo that's really neat.

1 Put the doll in a box on the top shelf of a closet. *[Helps them put away things after they use them.]*

2 Tie the doll in a laundry bag of filthy socks. *[Gives them a taste of their own penicillin.]*

3 Poke several broom bristles into the doll. Cover it with detergent. Then squeeze it in a mop wringer. *[Forces them to clean up after themselves.]*

4 Stick the doll's head in the spokes of a bicycle. Go for a ride. *[Teaches them the value of recycling.]*

5 Squirt the doll with shampoo, then rinse under hot water. *[Gets them to take a shower.]*

6 Cut open the doll, remove the stuffing, and boil it. Throw away the outer shell. *[Gives them a serious bath if the shower doesn't work.]*

IF ALL ELSE FAILS...
Have them sanitized for your protection.

SPELL

Your pants have rips
Your shirts have stains
Your shoes and socks
Give shocks and pains
Your breath is bad
You pick your nose
May every bath
Be by fire hose.

You're hosting a benefit for a key civic organization. This is an exclusive event—normally you wouldn't even be invited. Tires squeal. The snob arrives in a big car, handing you the keys and a dollar tip. Back inside, the snob sneers at your décor, spits out your wine, and makes snide comments about the wine stain in your white carpet. After picking the shrimp from the hors d'oeuvres, the snob refuses to donate anything to your "pathetic little charity," takes back the dollar, and storms out. **You want REVENGE!**

HE SNOB

DO THAT VOODOO

If you know people who think nothing is good enough, here's some voodoo that'll be good for them.

1 Sew the doll's mouth closed with twine or cheap thread. *[Keeps them from talking about all the expensive, exclusive things they own.]*

2 Wrap the doll in a piece of heavy wool and stick pins through the shoulders. *[Prevents them from giving you the cold shoulder and other snubs.]*

3 Smear glue on the doll, then cover it with bird seed. *[Forces them to own only things that are cheap, cheap, cheap.]*

4 Pin the head of the doll to its feet. *[Keeps them from sticking their nose in the air.]*

5 Take a branding iron to the doll's head. *[Discourages them from being brand conscious.]*

IF ALL ELSE FAILS...
Ask for their hand-me-downs.

CURSE

Good, better, best

Never take a rest

Spend, my friend

Until your money's end

And when you're broke

You still won't get the joke

You're in a pancake restaurant again (not that French restaurant you wanted) having French toast again (instead of crêpes). "Come on, try something new," you beg your stubborn spouse. Nothing doing. Back in the car, you point out the upcoming left turn. The stubborn one says, "We go straight." You present eight pieces of evidence to support your position. And still you go straight...straight into a construction site. As the car sinks in wet cement, guess who's standing on the hood, insisting the road signs were changed? **You want REVENGE!**

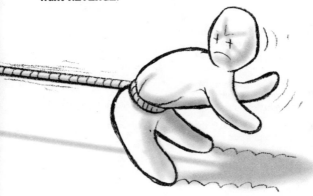

HE **STUBBORN**

Do That Voodoo

If you're stuck with a stick-in-the-mud, here's some voodoo to loosen them up.

1 Take a photo negative of the person, pin it to the doll, then hold it to a vacuum cleaner until the vacuum swallows the negative. *[Sucks all of the negative energy out of them.]*

2 Take the doll by the hand and twirl it quickly. *[Loosens them up for a good compromise.]*

3 Slit the doll's eyes and ears. *[Gets them to open their eyes and ears.]*

4 Make a slit in the back of the doll's head. Add extra stuffing. *[Expands their mind.]*

5 Cut off the doll's hand. *[Keeps them from shooting down all of your ideas.]*

6 Staple the doll to a Frisbee™ and throw it as far as possible. *[Makes them go away.]*

If All Else Fails...

Try dynamite. It will move them.

CHANT

You never bend
You never give
You take
Nobody's crap
The twig that
Never, ever yields
Will be the first
To snap

You're at work, doing what you do best, which happens to be waiting patiently for Friday afternoon while keeping a low profile. When the big boss makes the rounds, your manager makes a play. "Gee, boss, your hair looks great today." (It's the worst hairpiece you've ever seen.) "And I agree with your memo. Longer hours will make us more productive. In fact, I'm organizing a series of volunteers to work double shifts. On the weekends. For free." And then the Suck-Up points to you. The big boss smiles. **You want REVENGE!**

HE SUCK-UP

DO THAT VOODOO

If you know someone who gets ahead by going for the bottom, here's some voodoo that will really make them pucker.

1 Write the word YES on the doll's face, then cover it completely with hot wax. *[Seals in the urge to always say "yes."]*

2 Wrap tape tightly around the doll's face. Stick in a few pins. *[Wipes out that "can do" smile and makes them look bad.]*

3 Take an object that's symbolic of your job, and crush the doll with it. *[Makes them pick up your burden at work, instead of the boss's.]*

4 Staple the doll's legs together, and pour coffee all over the doll. *[Causes them to stumble and spill coffee on themselves as they try to serve others.]*

5 Tie a pen around the doll's back. *[Makes kneeling and bootlicking impossible. Also provides them with a spine.]*

IF ALL ELSE FAILS...

Get a promotion and enjoy the attention.

JINX

Smile that smile
Pay those dues
Kneel, and shine
The boss's shoes
Laugh and whistle
And when you're through
Don't get up
You'll shine mine, too

you're on the phone with family, fretting over a manufacturer's recall of Aunt Edna's heart and liver machine. Tensions are high. You get call waiting. There's an important call you need to take. A voice mangles your name: "We can offer you better phone service <u>and</u> a greener lawn." You slam down the phone, disconnecting everybody. **You want REVENGE!**

HE TELEMARKETER

DO THAT VOODOO

Here is the voodoo equivalent of *69, giving a call back (and payback) to the last person who rang you.

1 Lay the earpiece of the phone over the doll's head while they recite their sales pitch. *[Curses them to hear the echo of their own noisy voice.]*

2 Stick ten pins in the doll's chest—one for each digit on the phone. *[Causes chest pains when they call you, and lets you work in peace.]*

3 Wrap the curly telephone cord twice around the neck of your voodoo doll. *[Takes the wind from their voice box.]*

4 Stick a pin in each of the hands. *[Keeps their hands from dialing any more numbers.]*

5 Hang up and leave the receiver on top of the doll until that nasty sharp sound tells you the phone is off the hook. *[Gives them a headache, and gives you a few minutes when the phone won't ring again.]*

IF ALL ELSE FAILS...

Try calling the Attorney General's office.

CURSE

Selling insurance
Or credit card deals
Real estate bargains
And charity appeals
Your voice and your hands
May they freeze on the spot
So you'll never call
When dinner is hot

You're at your retirement party. After a lifetime of work as a voodoo consultant, it's time to hang up your dolls. You and your co-workers sit down to a nice dinner. Suddenly, a feeling comes over you. You freeze. You can't talk. You're being voodoo'd! Next, you find yourself walking over to your ex-assistant, handing over your gold watch, and signing over your pension check. Then you surrender the keys to your car. After everything you've done for this traitor! **You want REVENGE!**

E TRAITOR

DO THAT VOODOO

If someone you trust turns into a bust, here's some voodoo that's an absolute must.

1 Pin the doll's hands to its chest. *[Keeps them from pointing fingers at other people when the mistake is theirs.]*

2 Stick a knife in the back of the doll. *[Gives them a taste of their own medicine.]*

3 Whack the doll's head against your desk. *[Keeps them from stealing your job.]*

4 Whack the doll's head against your loved one. *[Keeps them from stealing your loved one.]*

5 Whack the doll's head against anything else you want to keep. *[You've really got to stay ahead of those traitors.]*

6 Fill your kitchen sink. Make a plank from a ruler and walk the doll along it. Push the doll overboard. *[Punishes them the way traitors are meant to be punished.]*

IF ALL ELSE FAILS...

If you can't beat them, too bad.

HEX

Finger pointer
Back stabber
Disappointer
Credit grabber
Coffin nail
Truth fearer
Your only pal
Will be the mirror

INDEX

READ THIS LAST

HOW THIS BOOK CAN HELP YOU

The voodoo in this book is symbolic revenge. It can make your anger go away. It can make you happy. It's a good substitute for *actual* revenge, which is impractical, messy, probably illegal, and worst of all, can get you caught. We've also heard there are ethical implications. Anything's possible.

HOW THIS BOOK CAN HURT YOU

For one thing, you can stick yourself with the pins. Don't do that. You can also do dangerous things to the doll that aren't smart, like setting it on fire or pouring poisons on it. (Please call our lawyers for a complete list of what not to do.)

If people find a voodoo doll with their name on it, you can get slapped silly or, worse, ostracized by people you don't even like. However, don't worry about conjuring vengeful evil spirits you can't control. Not with this book.

YOU'RE INVITED

We invite you to submit your own unique voodoo ceremonies for bad behavior. Who needs to be voodoo'd? And what awful things can you do to your doll?

Log on to **www.VoodooRevenge.com** and send your ideas. Write a whole page, or just do one voodoo, following the book's style. If you're victoriously vengeful, you'll get your revenge in the next book, a free copy, and we'll even mention your name. *If you dare.*

WWW.VOODOOREVENGE.COM